The safe use and handling of

FLAMMABLE LIQUIDS

HSE BOOKS

HS(G)140

ISBN 0 7176 0967 7

*This guidance is issued
by the Health and
Safety Executive.
Following the guidance
is not compulsory and
you are free to take
other action. But if you
do follow the guidance
you will normally be
doing enough to
comply with the law.
Health and safety
inspectors seek to
secure compliance with
the law and may refer
to this guidance as
illustrating good
practice.*

c o n

t e n t s

contents *continued*

preface

> *The guidance is aimed at those directly responsible for the safe use and handling of flammable liquids in all general work activities and in small-scale chemical processing*

This publication provides information on the fire and explosion hazards associated with flammable liquids, and sets out practical measures to protect people at work and others who may be affected by work activities involving flammable liquids. The guidance is aimed at those directly responsible for the safe use and handling of flammable liquids in all general work activities and in small-scale chemical processing. Safety specialists and trade organisations or associations may wish to use this book as a basis for more specific guidance for their own members.

THE OBJECTIVES OF THIS PUBLICATION ARE TO:

☛ increase the awareness of the potential fire and explosion hazards associated with flammable liquids;

☛ advise on safe operating procedures and precautions to reduce injuries and damage caused by fires and explosions while handling flammable liquids;

☛ give guidance on appropriate standards for plant and equipment:

☛ advise on the need for appropriate fire precautions, maintenance, training and good housekeeping where flammable liquids are handled or used.

Where a British Standard is quoted, any other national or international standard that provides an equivalent level of safety is acceptable. Harmonised European Standards that bear the preface BS EN may supersede some British Standards, and these are equally acceptable when published.

INTRODUCTION

1   This guidance book gives advice on the safe use of flammable liquids in general work activities, including batch or small scale chemical processing. It does not cover large-scale continuous processing plant in refineries, chemical works and similar premises. It is mainly concerned with fire and explosion hazards, although some general advice is given on health risks where this may be helpful.

2   This guidance will help assessment of the risks arising from the use and handling of flammable liquids. Assessment, by employers and the self-employed, of the risks to workers and others who may be affected by their activities is one of the requirements of the Management of Health and Safety at Work Regulations 1992[1]. A risk assessment will enable employers and others to decide on the appropriate measures to take to fulfil their statutory obligations. This publication also advises on how to comply with the relevant parts of the Health and Safety at Work etc Act 1974[2] at places where flammable liquids are used and, where applicable, with the Highly Flammable Liquids and Liquefied Petroleum Gases Regulations 1972[3] and other relevant legislation (see Appendix 1).

3   Legal requirements, guidance literature and the standards referred to in this guidance are listed in the reference section. They are subject to amendment from time to time. The glossary at the back of this book explains the particular terms used in this guidance.

SCOPE

4   In this guidance 'flammable liquid' means a liquid with a flashpoint of 55°C or below. This does not include liquids which when tested at 55°C in the manner described in Schedule 2 of the Highly Flammable Liquids and Liquefied Petroleum Gases Regulations 1972[3] do not support combustion, and which have a flashpoint equal to or more than 21°C and less than or equal to 55°C.

5   This definition for flammable liquid includes all liquids that are classified as flammable, highly flammable or extremely flammable for supply according to the Chemicals (Hazard Information and Packaging for Supply) Regulations 1994[4]. This definition also includes highly flammable liquids, petroleum spirit and petroleum mixtures as defined in the Highly Flammable Liquids and Liquefied Petroleum Gases Regulations 1972[3], the Petroleum (Consolidation) Act 1928[5], and the Petroleum (Mixtures) Order 1929[6] respectively.

6   The guidance is also relevant to liquids with a flashpoint above 55°C which are handled at temperatures above their flashpoint, as they may also present a fire and explosion hazard.

7   More detailed advice on the storage, carriage, loading and unloading, and spraying of flammable liquids; on the dispensing of petrol at filling stations; and on specific industries will be found in documents listed in the Further reading section. The advice in this book does not apply to flammable liquids which present special hazards requiring specific precautions, eg ethylene oxide, peroxides, and other liquids which carry a risk of rapid decomposition, polymerisation or spontaneous combustion.

8   The advice in this publication provides a suitable standard for the design of new installations and for major modifications to existing installations. It may be difficult to adopt all the recommendations at existing premises, but any improvements that are reasonably practicable should be made, taking into account the hazards at the site and the cost and feasibility of additional precautions. This document describes one way of achieving an adequate standard of safety. Individual circumstances, for both new and existing installations, may require variations from the recommendations, so alternative designs, materials and methods can be used, as long as they provide an equivalent level of safety. Advice on applying the guidance to specific sites can be obtained from the enforcing authority.

9   The handling of flammable liquids and the management of any released

vapours can have environmental consequences and may be subject to controls under the Environmental Protection Act 1990[7]. Although this guidance does not attempt to cover environmental issues, the advice it contains for safe use and handling of flammable liquids will generally also provide protection for the environment. However, some activities, such as reducing vapour levels by ventilation techniques, may require additional environmental controls; those involved in these activities are also advised to refer to specific guidance on these controls and on other environmental issues. Further guidance is available from HM Inspectorate of Pollution or from local authorities, who enforce the Environmental Protection Act.

HAZARDS

10   The main hazards from the use of flammable liquids are fire and explosion, involving either the liquid or the vapour given off from it. Fires or explosions are likely to occur when vapours or liquids are released from a controlled environment to areas where there may be an ignition source, or, alternatively, when an ignition source is introduced into a controlled environment. Common causes of such incidents include:

- lack of awareness of the properties of flammable liquids;
- operator error, due to lack of training;
- hot work on or close to flammable liquid containers;
- inadequate design of equipment;
- inadequate installation or maintenance;
- failure or malfunction of equipment;
- exposure to heat from a nearby fire;
- misuse of flammable liquids, for example, to burn waste materials or brighten fires;
- inadequate control of ignition sources;
- electrostatic discharges;
- heating materials above their auto-ignition temperature;
- dismantling or disposing of equipment containing flammable liquids.

Incidents involving flammable liquids commonly arise during transfer operations, including:

☞ movement from storage;

☞ decanting or dispensing;

☞ movement within premises;

☞ use in processes;

☞ disposal;

☞ emptying vehicle fuel tanks;

☞ dealing with spillages.

11   Combustion of liquids occurs when flammable vapours released from the surface of the liquid ignite. The amount of flammable vapour given off from a liquid, and therefore the extent of the fire or explosion hazard, depends largely on the temperature of the liquid, its volatility, how much of the surface area is exposed, how long it is exposed for, and air movement over the surface. Other physical properties of the liquid, such as flashpoint, auto-ignition temperature, viscosity, lower explosion limit and upper explosion limit, give further information as to how vapour/air mixtures may develop and also on the potential hazards.

12   Flashpoint is the lowest temperature at which a liquid gives off vapour in sufficient concentration to form a combustible mixture with air near the surface of the liquid. Generally, a liquid with a flashpoint below ambient temperature will give off a vapour that can mix with air and be ignited. Liquids with a flashpoint greater than ambient temperature are less likely to give off flammable concentrations of vapours unless they are heated, mixed with low flashpoint materials or released under pressure as a mist or spray. However, a material below its flashpoint can also be ignited when spread out as a thin film over a large area of ground or when spilled onto clothing. The explosion limits define the concentrations (normally by volume) of vapour/air mixtures at specified temperatures that will propagate a flame. Explosion limits vary greatly for different substances, but for many they are in the range of 1% to 10%.

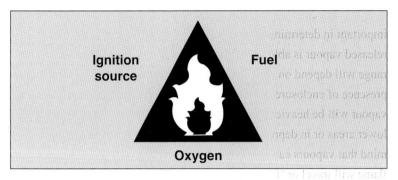

Figure 1 The Fire Triangle

13   Some materials such as water/solvent mixtures or emulsions only release vapours slowly. These materials can flash during a flashpoint determination and be assigned a flashpoint, but may not have the ability to sustain combustion at the temperatures encountered in normal use, though these may well be in excess of the measured flashpoint. Materials with a flashpoint above 21°C which do not support combustion when tested according to the method indicated in paragraph 4 are not normally considered to be a fire hazard. However, flammable vapours may build up in enclosed spaces above the liquid, and could explode if ignited.

14   The viscosity of the liquid is significant as it determines how far any spilt material will spread and therefore the size of any exposed surface. Solvents generally have a low viscosity and when spilt spread quickly, allowing a rapid build-up of vapours from the surface of the liquid. Some liquid formulations, such as paints and resins, may have a high viscosity; if they are spilt they spread and produce vapours more slowly than would the individual solvent constituents.

15   A flammable vapour/air mix is easily ignited by the external ignition sources discussed in paragraphs 45 to 62. Even if there are no external sources present the mixture may self-ignite if it is heated above its auto-ignition temperature. The properties of a flammable liquid should therefore be established (for example, from the relevant data sheet) before the material is used, so that adequate precautions can be taken. L62[8] contains further guidance on how to provide information.

16   The physical environment in which flammable liquids are handled is also important in determining how the hazards may develop. Whether the released vapour is able to build up to a concentration within its flammable range will depend on the ventilation at the surface of the liquid and on the presence of enclosures to trap or contain the vapours. In many cases the vapour will be heavier than air, and it will therefore tend to accumulate in lower areas or in depressions such as pits, gulleys and drains. Bear in mind that vapours can spread away from the liquid; if they are ignited the flame will travel or 'flash' back to the liquid.

17   Flammable liquids can also pose a health hazard if they are inhaled, ingested or come into contact with skin or eyes. Information on the health hazards of a particular liquid and on any specific precautions required should be obtained from the safety data sheet or from the supplier. The Control of Substances Hazardous to Health Regulations 1994[9] require employers to assess the risks from exposure to hazardous substances and the precautions needed. Paragraphs 68 and 69 give further details on health precautions.

PRECAUTIONS

Substitution

18   The use of low flashpoint liquids should be avoided whenever possible. Other liquids, which are either non-flammable or have a higher flashpoint, may provide suitable alternatives, but they may pose a risk to health or the environment. In such cases a judgement should be made which takes into account all the risks in the particular circumstances. Some halogenated hydrocarbons are considered non-flammable, and although in terms of their flammable properties they are not as dangerous as high flashpoint liquids, they can still burn or cause explosions in the presence of high energy sources such as a welding torch. These solvents are more accurately described as having reduced flammability rather than as being non-flammable, and they need to be considered accordingly.

Separation

19   Areas where flammable liquids are handled should normally be separated from other parts of the workroom by fire-resisting partitions (see paragraph 42 and Appendix 2). Care is needed to ensure partitions do not restrict escape routes or exits. Where partitions will require a change to existing escape routes or exits the enforcing authority for the general fire precautions (see paragraph 84) should be consulted. Areas where flammable liquids are used should also be fire-separated from areas where other flammable materials, of any type, are stored. Advice on the storage of dangerous substances in general is contained in HS(G)71[10]. Advice on the storage of flammable liquids in containers is provided in HS(G)51[11].

Dispensing and decanting

20   Dispensing and decanting should be carried out in a way which reduces spills and dangerous releases of flammable vapours. The need for these operations should be assessed and, where possible, minimised by the use of enclosed transfer systems (see paragraphs 36 and 37). If an enclosed system cannot be used, the containers should be designed to minimise spillage, release of vapour and the effects of fire. Small safety containers are available (see Figure 2) which incorporate the following features:

- metal or heavy-duty plastic construction;
- pouring and/or filling apertures sealed with self-closing spring loaded caps;
- pouring and/or filling apertures fitted with flame arresters;
- hoses or other aids when dispensing into small openings;
- carrying handles for containers with a capacity greater than approximately 2.5 litres.

Containers should be able to resist wear and tear in normal use and corrosion by the specific liquid being used. They should be strong enough to withstand being dropped. Plastic containers need to be compatible with the fluid that they are intended to contain. They should incorporate anti-static features so that any metal components in the transfer system, such as flame arresters or funnels, cannot build up incendive electrostatic charges. The use of containers approved by a recognised testing and approval organisation is recommended.

Figure 2 Examples of safety containers

21   Open-topped cans and buckets are not suitable for handling or storing flammable liquids as they increase the risk of spillage and the release of vapours. Drums should be provided with secure closures that can withstand the expected handling conditions without leaking. Drums with large removable ends are not normally suitable for flammable liquids. Open-ended drums or receptacles with fitting lids or covers may be adequate for viscous liquids such as paints, provided the container is not easily tipped over. Drums and cans should always be opened so that they can easily be closed again, not by punching holes in the cap or in the drum wall.

22   Decanting or transfer from one container to another should normally be carried out away from the area where the liquid is stored, and preferably in the open air or in a separate, well ventilated room, so that any spillage and possible fire cannot involve the stored materials. When pouring manually from or into small containers, use a funnel to

minimise spillage. Spill trays, drip cans or other means to contain spillages should be provided where decanting or dispensing is carried out, and containers should be bonded together or earthed - see paragraph 48. Also consider providing flame arresters in the container vent to reduce evaporation and to prevent an explosion inside the container in case of an external fire. Where flammable liquids are routinely dispensed from 210 litre drums the following alternative methods are recommended:

☞ **Using drum safety taps in conjunction with safety vents**
Drum taps should be made of non-combustible material and be self-closing. Safety vents prevent excess pressure or vacuum building up inside the drum and stop any ignition source from flashing back into the drum. A safety vent also reduces the likelihood of a drum exploding if it is engulfed by fire. When dispensing into containers with small apertures, use a funnel or taps fitted with small-diameter hoses to minimise spillage.

Figure 3
System for decanting from 210 litre drum using safety tap

☞ **Using small portable drum pumps**

Pumps ought to fit closely into the drum to minimise release of vapours, but they also need to be able to relieve pressure in the event of a fire. Flexible hoses need to be electrically conducting. If an electric pump is used, the electrical equipment should be constructed to a suitable explosion-protection standard - see paragraph 46.

Figure 4
System for decanting from 210 litre drum using hand pump

23   All containers should be labelled according to their purpose, so that people who use them or come into contact with them are aware of their contents and the hazards associated with them. Flammable liquids that are being handled in their original containers will already be suitably labelled in accordance with the Chemicals (Hazard Information and Packaging for Supply) Regulations 1994[4]. Where liquids are transferred into secondary containers for in-house use, the containers should be labelled to indicate their contents and the possible hazards. For

flammable liquids the fire hazard may be shown by labelling conforming to BS 5378[12] or by a red diamond showing the fire logo and the words 'flammable liquid'. Containers filled from bulk storage tanks or vessels may be labelled in accordance with the requirements for those tanks or vessels. The Highly Flammable Liquids and Liquefied Petroleum Gases Regulations 1972[3] require tanks or vessels used for storing highly flammable liquids to be clearly and boldly marked 'highly flammable' or 'flashpoint below 32°C', or to indicate flammability in some other way. Containers that have been emptied but not gas freed are also potentially dangerous and should be handled, stored and labelled as if they were full.

24   In certain circumstances it may be acceptable to transfer flammable liquids in or near to the storage facilities. This should only be done if an assessment of the fire risks has been carried out and precautions taken to prevent any incident during dispensing from escalating to involve the bulk liquids. In these cases precautions would include:

- the exclusion of all ignition sources;
- control and retention of possible spillages to prevent them spreading around stored materials;
- controllable transfer systems;
- good ventilation.

Any additional fire precautions can also be taken into account in assessing the safety of a particular dispensing operation.

Pipework

25   All parts of piping systems, including valve seals and flange gaskets, should be made from material compatible with the liquids being handled. They should be constructed in accordance with an appropriate standard, for example, the American National Standards Institute Standard B31.3[13] with Engineering Equipment and Materials Users Association Supplement 153[14]. Plastic or other similar materials are normally only used if there are particular reasons, such as product

purity, and if an equivalent standard of construction can be achieved. Plastic pipes, as well as being more vulnerable to fire, may also cause greater electrostatic problems - see paragraphs 47 to 49. Where possible welded joints should be used rather than flanges, to minimise the risk of leakage, although piping with a diameter of 50 mm or less may have screwed joints. Joints and connections should be kept to a minimum and should not be positioned where they might leak onto electrical equipment, hot surfaces or other sources of ignition, or where they might prevent the use of an escape route.

26   Pressure from thermal expansion of liquids can build up in pipework in which liquids may be trapped, for example, between shut-off valves. Prevent damage to pipework and dangerous releases of flammable liquids as a result of over-pressurisation by assessing the likelihood and consequences of thermal expansion and designing the system to withstand the pressure rises. Alternatively, fit hydrostatic relief valves. Relief valves should normally discharge back to the storage tank, but they may also discharge via a line to a safe place such as a sump or other vessel designed for the recovery or disposal of flammable liquids.

27   Ideally, pipe runs should be in the open air rather than inside buildings. Pipework should be sized and routed to restrict the contents to a minimum (consistent with pressure-drop requirements). It should be positioned or protected to minimise the risk of impact damage, particularly from vehicles - barriers or bollards may be needed. Pipework supports need to be designed to suit the piping layout and to withstand any anticipated vibration and other stresses (see BS 3974)[15]. BS CP 1710[16] recommends the use of a suitable marking system to identify the contents of individual pipe runs. Marking of pipework is particularly important at filling and discharge points or where there is likely to be confusion with other piping systems. Use different filling nozzle designs for different materials to avoid confusion.

28   Pipe runs in buildings should normally be in the open and should not pass through hazard areas such as furnace or boiler rooms. They may need protection from other localised hot surfaces or heating systems. Routeing

pipework through ducts can cause problems in detection and control of leaks, and can allow vapours to travel from one area to another. Ducts should therefore only be used for pipework when there is no safe practical alternative. In this case the ducts should be constructed to a specified standard of fire-resistance, provided with fire stops at suitable intervals and adequately ventilated. Where ducts or pipes pass through a fire-resisting structure, any gaps between the duct or pipe and the structure should be fire-stopped. Pipework should not be installed in ducts used for heating or ventilation. BS 8313[17] gives further guidance on the design of ducts.

Figure 5
Pipework with marking system for identification

29   Pipework may be installed underground, although this presents

difficulties with leak prevention, inspection and repair. The pipework should be laid in a shallow concrete or masonry-lined trench provided with load bearing covers. The design of the trench should prevent water or moisture accumulating around the pipework and allow for inspection of the pipework and in particular any joints. The design should also allow for any extra loading imposed, for example, by vehicles. Do not use the same trench for piping carrying corrosive or reactive materials such as oxygen or chlorine. The route of the trench should be recorded and permanently marked at the surface.

30   The routeing of electric cables in the same trench as pipework should normally be avoided, but where this is not practicable the cables must be prevented from acting as a possible ignition source for any vapours within the trench. Assess the areas inside the trench that present hazards because of pipework joints or from other hazardous areas connected to the trench. Select and install the cables and associated electrical equipment according to BS 5345[18] or other equivalent standards (ie the draft harmonised European Code of Practice prEN 50154)[19]. Consider sealing the trench from process areas or other hazardous areas to limit the spread of flammable vapours inside the trench or into safe areas.

31   Underground pipes that must be buried for security or other reasons need protection against corrosion. Buried pipes should be manufactured from stainless steel or galvanised iron covered with a proprietary anti-corrosion paint or tape. Alternatively, they should be provided with secondary containment (see also paragraph 32). All underground joints should be welded, unless welding is inappropriate for corrosion protection or other reasons. In these cases screwed connections are acceptable. Flanged joints are only acceptable if they are situated in a manhole chamber which has been sealed to prevent any leaks of flammable liquid draining into the ground. Buried pipework should be encased in sulphate-resisting concrete. If it is thick enough and bedded properly under the pipe it will prevent damage to the pipeline from any anticipated loads. All buried pipework that cannot be inspected or is not provided with continual leak monitoring will require regular leak testing.

32   Other pipework systems manufactured from glass-reinforced plastic, polypropylene or other plastics and having secondary containment can be used underground as long as they are compatible with the materials being handled. These systems should be buried in pea shingle or sand in accordance with the manufacturer's instructions. The space between the pipe and its secondary containment should be monitored for leaks. Again, concrete overlay or load bearing covers will be needed to provide protection from traffic or other additional loading.

Flexible hoses

33   Flexible hoses should only be used where rigid piping is unsuitable, such as at filling connections or where vibration is a problem. Hoses should be made to a standard suitable for the application and should be compatible with the liquids handled. They should be adequately supported (for example, by slings or saddles) so that the bend radius is not less than the minimum recommended by the manufacturer. When they are not in use, protect the hoses from accidental damage, extremes of temperature and direct sunlight. Inspect them on each day they are used for signs of leaks, wear and mechanical damage, and examine and pressure-test them at least once a year according to the manufacturer's recommendations. It is good practice to provide blank ends for additional sealing of couplings that are frequently broken and remade. Hoses should be electrically continuous or bridged with an earthing cable to avoid electrostatic charging.

Ancillary equipment

34   Pumps, motors and other equipment forming part of a piping system should be sited in a well-ventilated place, preferably in the open air, with weather protection where necessary. Such ancillary equipment should be situated outside of any bunds for storage tanks. Small leaks from pumps need to be contained by a low sill or drained to a safe place. Where natural ventilation is inadequate, for example in underground pumprooms, mechanical ventilation should be provided (see paragraphs 63 to 67). Interlocks should be fitted so that the pumps

cannot be operated unless the ventilation is working satisfactorily. If the non-operation of a pump could cause a greater hazard than a lack of ventilation in the pump room, a clearly audible alarm should be linked to the ventilation system.

Isolation

35   There should be suitable valves within the pipework system for isolating the supply after use, during maintenance and in the event of an emergency. Consider providing shut-off valves in the following locations:

- ☛ at the external supply point;
- ☛ externally at the point of entry into the building;
- ☛ at the beginning of each branch from a main supply line;
- ☛ near each work position or item of plant supplied by the line, where that position is more than 10 m from a valve provided to comply with the last bullet point;
- ☛ where pipework passes through an internal wall, partition or floor.

All valves should be clearly marked and designed to achieve a rapid shut-down of flow. Valves may be manual or automatic, but automatic valves should be installed to be fail-safe.

Transfer systems

36   Flammable liquids should ideally be handled in enclosed systems, using pipework, pumps and closed vessels. The equipment should be suitable for the liquids being handled, and, where appropriate, should be designed and installed to a suitable British Standard or equivalent. Where liquids are transferred by gas pressure, nitrogen or another inert gas, or vacuum may be used. Do not use compressed air as it can create an explosive vapour/air mixture inside the transfer vessel. The gas should be controlled to the lowest practicable pressure within the system. Means for rapid isolation of the pressure source and venting of the pipeline or pressure source to a safe place should be provided. It is not advisable to fill or empty portable containers by gas pressure as it is difficult to

control the flow adequately and there is a risk of pressurising the container, causing it to rupture violently. Gravity flow is also difficult to control, except with cans or small drums. Avoid it unless suitable additional safeguards are provided, such as automatic or remotely-operated shut-off valves.

Process areas

37 Design and operate process areas to minimise risks: using pipework systems and closed vessels rather than handling liquids in containers and open tanks will restrict the amount of liquid open to the air and reduce the risks from released vapours. Liquids should not be heated above the required working temperature, as the amount of vapour produced increases as the temperature rises.

38 Filling lines should end as near as possible to the bottom of the vessel, to minimise the free fall of liquid and the generation of static electricity - see paragraph 49. The line should be designed to prevent any syphoning from the filled vessel. Fitting automatic prevention devices will reduce the likelihood of overfilling vessels with flammable liquids, particularly if the person controlling the filling operation is at some distance from the vessel. These devices may take the form of:

- ☞ an overflow;
- ☞ a pre-set meter;
- ☞ a fixed volume batch tank;
- ☞ or a level detector linked to a pump or valve.

Where a high-level alarm system is fitted it should be triggered at one level to alert the operator to shut off the valve or pump, and at a second level to shut it off automatically if the operator takes no action. Before installing automatic shut-off valves, assess whether shock loading within the supply line could result in any hazards. Process vessels or areas need a means of containing spillages, such as a bund or retaining sill. The drains from bunded areas should not feed directly into the public system.

39   Vent pipes should normally be provided on process plant. These will
        prevent flammable and toxic vapours released during filling and
        processing from accumulating in work areas and direct them away from
        plant operators and possible ignition sources. Vent pipes should
        terminate outside buildings, well away from possible ignition sources,
        so that any vapours can be rapidly dispersed and not re-enter the source
        building or other buildings. Ideally, vent pipes should discharge
        vertically upwards, but horizontal discharge may be acceptable. The
        vent pipe should normally finish at least 5 m above ground level; 3 m
        from building openings, boundaries and sources of ignition; and away
        from building eaves and other obstructions. These distances may,
        however, vary according to the site layout.

40   There may also be environmental restrictions on the positioning of
        vents and exhaust ducts (see paragraph 65) - refer to Process Guidance
        Notes issued under the Environmental Protection Act (EPA)[7]. In
        particular, Process Guidance Notes issued under EPA may require vent
        pipes from certain processes to terminate at least 3 m above roof level.
        Vent pipes should be big enough to prevent over-pressurisation of the
        plant from material additions and other process operations. The vent
        pipes may also have to be designed to take into account any exothermic
        reactions, but this requirement is outside the scope of this current
        guidance book. For small open process vessels where materials are
        added manually, local exhaust ventilation may be more suitable than
        fixed vent pipes.

41   On vessels containing liquids with a flashpoint of 21°C or below, or for
        other liquids processed above their flashpoint, the vent outlet should be
        fitted with a flame arrester, unless a pressure-vacuum valve is used or
        unless the liquid is liable to polymerise or otherwise block the arrester.
        Flame arresters should be designed to BS 7244[20], and maintained to
        prevent blockage by paint, rust or other materials.

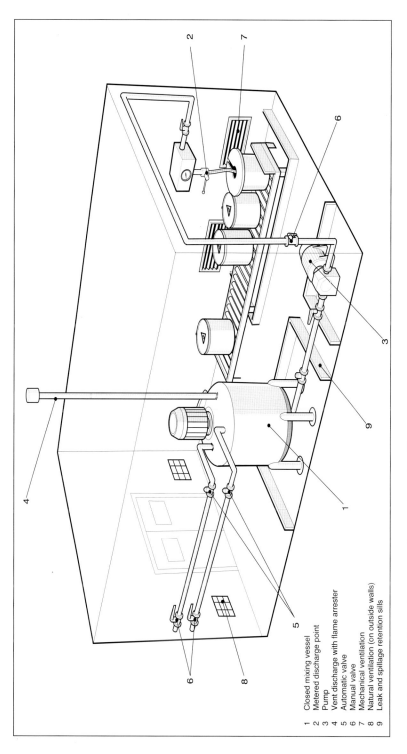

1 Closed mixing vessel
2 Metered discharge point
3 Pump
4 Vent discharge with flame arrester
5 Automatic valve
6 Manual valve
7 Mechanical ventilation
8 Natural ventilation (on outside walls)
9 Leak and spillage retention sills

Figure 6 Diagram illustrating systems in a work area handling flammable liquids

Figure 7 Examples of special purpose containers for flammable liquids

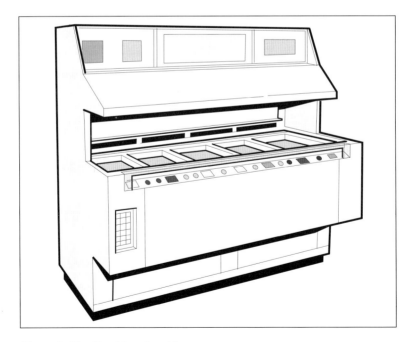

Figure 8 Ventilated 'wet bench'

42   Operations such as mixing, filling, coating and cleaning should be done in a room or cabinet set aside for the purpose. Where vapour may enter the atmosphere during any operation, adequate natural or mechanical ventilation should be provided to remove it. The ventilation source should be as close to the vapour source as possible - see paragraphs 63 to 67. If the concentration of vapour is liable to exceed the lower flammable limit, the process will need to be enclosed in a fire-resisting, mechanically ventilated structure. If this is not possible, the workroom itself should be a fire-resisting structure (see Appendix 2) and be mechanically ventilated. Figure 6 shows an example of a suitable work area. Specific advice on small-scale paint mixing systems in motor body repair and re-finishing is contained in HS(G)67[21].

43   Take care when using flammable liquids for cleaning machinery, equipment or articles, particularly by manual methods. The use of open tanks of volatile liquids for dipping components, etc, should be avoided. If it cannot be avoided, use special safety rinse/dip/bench cans. These cans are normally fitted with a flame arrester and/or self-closing lids. It is preferable to use non-flammable liquids, or liquids with a high flashpoint. Carry out the cleaning operation in a well ventilated area or cabinet and apply the liquid in small quantities. Figure 8 shows an example of a ventilated 'wet bench' suitable for cleaning and other operations involving the manual application of solvents. Large components should be cleaned in specially designed cleaning stations. It is advisable to apply the fluid using a pump producing a gentle non-jetting or spraying stream of liquid, with flow rates as low as possible. Avoid using heated solvents or jetting techniques unless the proposed cleaning temperature and equipment have been shown not to present a risk of fire or explosion with a particular solvent.

44   Keep no more than the minimum amount of flammable liquid in workrooms, usually no more than a half-day's or one shift's supply. Containers of flammable liquid needed for current work should be kept closed when not in use. They should be kept in suitable cabinets or bins in designated areas away from the immediate processing area. Containers which are nominally empty or are not needed for current work should be returned to the appropriate store (see HS(G)51[11] for further advice on cabinets, bins and stores). Containers at the workplace should:

- be as small as practicable;
- provide resistance to impact damage;
- be able to withstand damage and wear in normal use;
- resist chemical attack by their contents.

Proprietary safety containers are recommended (see paragraph 20). Use suitable cradles, trolleys or powered handling equipment for handling drums and other large containers to minimise the risk of spillages and injury to workers. During transport containers should be securely closed and where necessary secured so that they cannot fall off. Only authorised routes should be used when transporting the containers.

SOURCES OF IGNITION

45   Sources of ignition should normally be excluded from areas where flammable liquids are handled. Common sources of ignition are:

- naked flames, including welding and cutting equipment;
- smoking;
- electrical lighting, power circuits and equipment which are not flameproof or intrinsically safe in construction;
- processes and vehicles that involve friction or the generation of sparks;
- hot surfaces;
- static electricity.

Electrical equipment

46   Areas where electrical equipment is installed and where flammable vapour may be present can be classified into hazardous zones - see Appendix 3. Areas outside these zones are classified as non-hazardous. Where possible electrical equipment should be located in non-

hazardous areas. The Electricity at Work Regulations 1989[22] require electrical equipment which may be exposed to any flammable substance to be constructed or protected to prevent danger arising from such exposure. To comply with these Regulations and to prevent flammable vapours igniting, any electrical equipment installed or introduced into hazardous areas should be constructed to a suitable explosion-protected equipment standard (that is, an appropriate British Standard or equivalent). Advice on selecting, installing and maintaining explosion-protected electrical equipment is given in BS 5345[18] and in a short guide published by the Institution of Chemical Engineers[23]. Selecting the correct and safe electrical equipment entails:

- identifying the correct hazardous zone;
- establishing the appropriate gas group for the flammable liquids involved;
- confirming the maximum surface temperature ('T' number) of all electrical components.

Electrostatic charging

47   Precautions should be taken to prevent vapours being ignited by the discharge of static electricity. The movement of process liquids, for example, during pumping, emptying, filling and spraying, can cause electrostatic build-up. Movement of other materials, such as powders or a printing web, or cleaning operations, can also create electrostatic hazards. Non-conducting footwear and clothing made of synthetic fibres can cause incendive electrostatic sparks, especially if they are worn in areas with non-conducting floors.

48   To protect against electrostatic build-up all metal (or other conducting) components must be adequately earthed before any liquid flow begins. All fixed equipment used to handle flammable liquids should be electrically bonded together and adequately earthed. Check earth continuity regularly (at least annually - see BS 7430)[24]. Earthing contacts should be maintained and kept clean. Portable containers should also be earthed before use with bonding clips connected by a

wire to the fixed earthed plant or by some other equally effective
method. Bear in mind any unearthed metal components in transfer
systems, such as in valves, dispenser heads or sections of piping: these
may need additional earthing straps. Other unearthed components may
not be so obvious, or may result from poor maintenance. If uninsulated
wire reinforcement, in damaged pipe lagging, for example, is left
exposed it may build up electrostatic charges if it is subjected to steam
from leaking joints. If hoses are used, they should be electrically
continuous and bonded to both parts of the plant.

Figure 9 Photograph showing copper bonding on glass pipework, courtesy of
the Institute of Chemical Engineers (reproduced from the training package on
controlling electrostatic hazards).

49   Static electricity generated by flammable liquids should be reduced by
avoiding the free fall of liquids and restricting pumping speeds. For
liquids with conductivity up to and including 50 pS/m (pico
Siemens/metre) the flow velocity in a pipe where a second phase may
be present (a second phase could be a gas or a solid, or an immiscible
liquid such as water) should not exceed 1 m/s. Water may be present
even if it has not been deliberately introduced (for example,

condensate) and so a flow velocity above 1 m/s should only be considered if this is not a possibility. BS 5958[25] offers further advice for higher velocities. Splash filling of containers and process vessels should be avoided. Anti-static additives can be used to increase the conductivity of flammable liquids with a conductivity less than 50 pS/m.

50   Take particular care when adding dry powders to vessels containing flammable liquids. The movement of dry powders and other solids over insulated materials such as plastics can quickly cause incendive electrostatic sparks. Dry powders should not be added to process vessels containing flammable vapours using plastic scoops or plastic chutes, nor should they be discharged from plastic bags: if the vapours ignite, flames will be emitted from the vessel manhole directly onto workers. Consider removing workers from vulnerable positions and adopting the following measures to reduce the possibility of build-up of static and/or preventing the occurrence of flammable atmospheres:

☞   mechanical transfer systems;

☞   double-valved hopper systems;

☞   use of conducting plastic liner with drum earthing clip or with good earthing of operator;

☞   airlock and nitrogen purging;

☞   charging solids before solvent addition (check vapours from previous use);

☞   wet or slurry solid before addition;

☞   addition of solvents with a high conductivity before ones with a low conductivity if both are to be present.

51   Additional precautions include the use of anti-static footwear (to BS 5145[26] and BS 7193[27]), and anti-static clothing and floors. BS 5958[25] gives general advice on the control of static electricity and the determination of electrostatic properties.

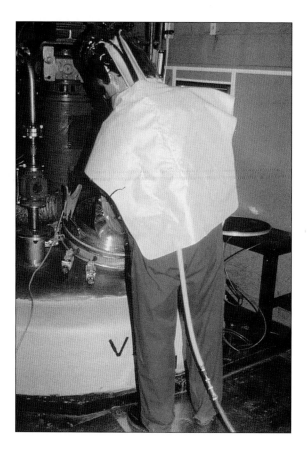

Figure 10 Operator charging reactor - note earth clip on manhole, earthed metal standing plate and antistatic footwear, courtesy of the Institute of Chemical Engineers (reproduced from the training package on controlling electrostatic hazards).

Friction sparks

52   Flammable vapour may be ignited by friction sparks. These can be generated by tools (hand-operated or power-driven), or by operations involving rubbing or impact. Special tools made of nickel-aluminium bronze or similar alloys may reduce sparking, but pieces of grit or tramp metal becoming embedded in working surfaces can present problems. Spark-resistant tools need to be inspected regularly and the surfaces re-dressed as necessary. The use of such tools is good practice, but do not rely on them alone in areas where flammable vapour may

occur: as far as possible, remove flammable liquids, residues and vapour before carrying out operations that may cause a spark.

53   Light alloys such as aluminium can cause sparking when struck a glancing blow on rusty steelwork. A smear of such an alloy on a rusty surface can also create a very hot spark if struck by another piece of steel, for example, a hammer. Identify where such metals are in use, so that procedures can be controlled in areas where flammable materials may be present and where there is a risk of impact. Aluminium powders in paints can cause similar problems, and their use in areas where flammable materials are present should also be controlled.

Protection of vehicles

54   Lift trucks and similar vehicles working in areas where flammable vapour may be present should be protected to an appropriate standard. Where only liquids with a flashpoint above 32°C are present, vehicle protection is not needed, as long as the liquids are not heated above their flashpoint, either directly or indirectly, nor likely to be released as a mist or spray. Guidance Note PM 58[28] provides further advice on the use and protection of vehicles.

Space heating

55   Workrooms in which flammable liquids are handled should preferably be heated by indirect means, for example, radiators fed by hot water pipes. Where hot water radiators cannot be used, electrically heated radiators may be used, providing they have been selected according to, and comply with, BS 5345[18]. Do not use heating which could be a source of ignition. The temperature of exposed surfaces should not exceed the auto-ignition temperature of any of the flammable liquids in use. In all cases heating systems should be protected against the build-up of flammable residues on hot surfaces. Do not use portable heaters unless they comply with BS 5345[18]. Combustion air for fuel fired heaters should not be drawn from areas which could contain flammable vapours.

Hot work

56   A major cause of incidents is hot work (welding, cutting or similar
      operations) carried out on vessels containing flammable vapour or
      liquid residues. Hot work should only be done under controlled
      conditions using a permit-to-work system. This will include following
      site rules and instructions, and operating only when authorised by a
      responsible person. Hot work must not be carried out on an item that
      contains or has contained flammable liquid or vapour until the item is
      made safe.

57   Before hot work is carried out, drain off any flammable liquid. Gas free
      the vessel, and thoroughly clean and inspect it to ensure all residues
      have been removed. Gas freeing alone is not enough, as residues of
      heavy materials may give off flammable vapours when heated, and
      apparently 'empty' containers or vessels may contain small amounts of
      unseen liquids at the bottom or in crevices and seams. An alternative
      technique is to inert the vessel by filling it with water, nitrogen foam or
      nitrogen. Take great care throughout the operation to ensure that no
      voids containing flammable vapours can occur in the vessel.

58   A competent person should monitor the atmosphere with a suitable gas
      detector as part of the overall operation, to show the vessel is safe for
      hot work. Carry out this monitoring as proof of gas freeing, and also,
      when using gas inerting techniques, both before and during the hot
      work operation. If water is used, prevent pressure building up by
      providing a vent for steam. Wherever possible the item should be taken
      to the workshop or a similar safe area, for both the cleaning/inerting
      operation and the hot work. Guidance Note CS 15[29], and the Oil
      Industry Advisory Committee document on permit-to-work
      procedures[30] give further advice on preparing plant for hot work, and on
      the use of permits.

Cold cutting

59   Consider using 'cold cutting' techniques as an alternative to hot work,

particularly during demolition work, as they can significantly reduce the risk of fires and explosions. Cold cutting methods include using:

- hydraulic or pneumatic powered cutters, nibblers, drills and saws;
- pneumatic chisels;
- high pressure water jetting.

With some cold cutting techniques the temperature and the possibility of sparks can be further reduced by applying water or other non-flammable liquids at the cutting edge. These methods may not completely remove the risk of ignition as, for example, pneumatic chisels can create friction sparks and water jetting may build up an electrostatic charge under certain circumstances.

60   Before using cold cutting methods, therefore, consider the precautions discussed in paragraph 57 to control the formation of flammable atmospheres as well as the ignition energies of any flammable liquid vapours or solid residues. Cold cutting reduces the frequency and strength of possible ignition sources and the evaporation of any remaining flammable materials that are contaminating the plant. In particular it prevents flammable atmospheres forming from high flashpoint liquids, including those with a flashpoint above 55°C. These have been known to cause serious accidents as a result of the rapid vaporisation of the liquid during hot work with an oxyacetylene flame.

61   Other cutting methods using grinders or disc cutters, although not strictly classified as hot work, still produce a significant number of sparks that can easily ignite flammable vapours. Grinders and disc cutters should therefore only be used on plant that has contained flammable materials after carefully assessing the hazards and the required precautions.

Smoking

62   Do not allow smoking in places where flammable liquids are handled. Notices prohibiting smoking and naked lights should be clearly displayed in these areas. It is recommended that signs comply with BS 5378[12]. Any

area set aside for smoking should be located in a safe place, and clearly defined and signposted. Provide adequate receptacles (preferably sand-filled) so that people can dispose of their smoking materials safely before they enter no-smoking areas.

VENTILATION

63   All areas where flammable liquids are handled should be adequately ventilated to dilute any released vapours to a safe level. The ventilation system needs to be capable of providing at least six complete air changes per hour. Whatever its capacity it should ensure that the amount of vapour in any work area is not only diluted to well below its flammable limit, but also reduced to a level below the relevant occupational exposure limit. (Guidance note EH 40[31] gives advice on occupational exposure limits.) In some cases good natural ventilation positioned predominantly at low level plus some at high level may be enough, but in others mechanical ventilation and/or local exhaust ventilation will be needed.

64   Where a booth or cabinet is needed to control vapour, the airflow rate into all openings in the enclosure should be about 1 m/s to prevent vapours entering the work area. The ventilation to booths, cabinets and other enclosed equipment should normally be designed to maintain the vapours at below 25% of their Lower Explosion Limit (LEL). Separate guidance on spraying flammable liquids is provided in Guidance Note EH 9[32], and on ovens and similar heated enclosures containing flammable vapours in HS(G)16[33]. Materials that may present health risks will require a higher standard of ventilation and additional precautions (see paragraph 68).

65   Ventilation systems should exhaust to a safe place in the open air, at least 3 m above ground level, at least 3 m from building openings, boundaries and sources of ignition; and away from building eaves and other obstructions. Vent ducts should be arranged so that vapours cannot condense and collect at low points within the ducts. Additional requirements for positioning exhausts from ventilation systems may

also be found in Process Guidance Notes issued under the Environmental Protection Act[7] (see paragraph 40).

66   Electric motors used in ventilation ducting should not be situated in the path of the vapour being extracted. Centrifugal or bifurcated fans can be used, or a motor situated in a safe area can be connected to a fan by a belt drive. Fans made from non-sparking materials provide an additional precaution against friction sparks. The ductwork itself should be fire-resisting - see Appendix 2.

67   Where the failure of an extraction system would entail a flammable concentration of vapour in the plant or an escape of toxic vapour, fit an airflow detector in the ducting (such as a differential pressure switch) linked to an alarm. Where it is reasonably practicable, the detector should also be interlocked with the vapour-producing process.

HEALTH PRECAUTIONS

68   Many of the recommendations in the preceding paragraphs will, if they are properly implemented, control health risks as well as the fire hazard of flammable liquids. However, additional precautions may be needed, in order to comply with the Control of Substances Hazardous to Health Regulations 1994[9]. Guidance on these Regulations is in the Approved Codes of Practice entitled *General COSHH ACoP, Carcinogens ACoP* and *Biological agents ACoP:Control of Substances Hazardous to Health Regulations 1994*[34].

69   Detailed consideration of these aspects is beyond the scope of this guidance, but the principles of enclosure ventilation and maintenance of equipment apply generally. The aim should always be to prevent exposure to liquids or their vapours, for example, by substitution where possible, or to control adequately any inevitable release. Provide precautions against skin and eye contact, such as gloves, protective clothing and goggles where it is not possible to control the release at source. Consider making available eye wash and emergency decontamination/deluge showers.

MAINTENANCE

70   Many incidents involving flammable liquids occur during maintenance and repairs, when pipelines are opened up, vessels are entered, hot work is carried out, or plant and buildings are modified. The risks increase if the work is done by staff or outside contractors with little knowledge of the plant or of the hazards associated with flammable liquids. Only employ experienced contractors, and ensure that they become familiar with the plant before starting work. The Health and Safety at Work etc Act 1974[2] places duties to ensure safe working practices on both the company using the services and the contractor.

71   It is essential that no maintenance work is done until:

- the potential hazards of the work have been clearly identified and assessed;
- the precautions needed have been specified in detail;
- the necessary safety equipment has been provided;
- adequate and clear instruction has been given to all those concerned.

When appropriate, a permit-to-work system should be used to control maintenance operations. Further advice on preventing accidents during maintenance is contained in HSE's publication *Dangerous maintenance - a study of maintenance accidents and how to prevent them*[35].

72   As far as possible all flammable or combustible materials should be removed from the work area. Isolate vessels and pipework from all sources of liquid or vapour, drain and, where necessary, flush them. Do not rely on valves for isolation other than for initial isolation as they may leak or be opened inadvertently. Make a detailed study of the plant layout and the maintenance work involved, and ensure isolation by fitting spade pieces, or by removing pipe sections and blanking off the open ends, as appropriate. Take extra care where orifice plates are fitted to reduce liquid flow as these may be confused with spade pieces. See also paragraph 57, on preparation for hot work.

HOUSEKEEPING

73   Housekeeping is fundamental to safety, so maintain a good standard at all times. Deal with spills and leaks promptly, using, for example, inert absorbent material which can be scooped up into a metal container for removal. Contain large spillages as far as possible, evacuate the area and post warning notices. Open external doors and windows to improve ventilation. Additional precautions may be needed to prevent spills entering the drains, unless the drains themselves are fitted with an interceptor system. Only use electrical equipment such as fans and portable pumps if it has been constructed to a suitable explosion-protection equipment standard. Do not operate electrical switches unless they are similarly protected.

74   Take care when dealing with spillages not to allow workers or their clothing to come into direct contact with the flammable liquid. This would expose them to a serious fire risk. For some spills it may be advisable to call the Fire Brigade as a precaution, or so that they can provide assistance in dealing with the spill. As part of the emergency planning procedures (see paragraph 89), discuss with the Fire Brigade beforehand their involvement in any incident.

75   Place cleaning rags and other items contaminated with liquid in a metal bin, suitably labelled and fitted with a self-closing metal lid. Empty bins at least daily as they not only present a fire hazard, but they may undergo spontaneous combustion, especially if their contents are contaminated with paint residues. Special bins are available which allow air to circulate beneath and around them to aid cooling. Contaminated clothing should be changed promptly, even if it appears to have dried, as flammable vapour can remain in clothing for a long time and it can be easily ignited, for example, by standing close to a heater or from smoking materials.

76   Processes should be designed and operated to minimise flammable residues building up on work surfaces, walls, etc. Remove any residues regularly, preferably without the use of solvents. Where solvents are

necessary, choose those with the least flammable or toxic properties and apply to small sections at a time. Good ventilation is essential during this work, and sources of ignition should be excluded.

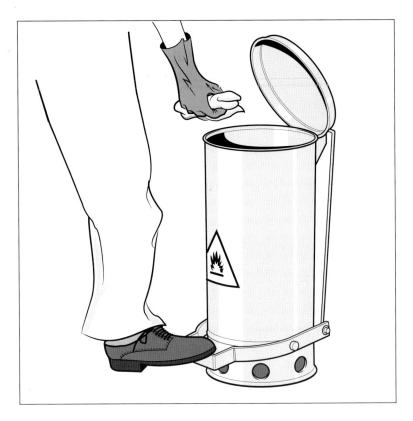

Figure 11   Examples of self closing container for cloths contaminated with solvents

DISPOSAL OF FLAMMABLE LIQUIDS

77   Waste liquids will generally need to be stored and handled according to the same standards as the flammable liquids from which they were derived. They will also be subject to the same legislation, unless their physical properties have been significantly altered by the processing. If, for example, the storage of the original flammable liquid required a licence from the Petroleum Licensing Authority, the waste material may also be subject to the same licence and conditions

78   Dispose of waste liquids safely, taking account of the need to prevent
      pollution. Never put waste liquid into public drains or watercourses.
      When in doubt, consult the local waste disposal authority.

Figure 12   Example of system for waste solvent collection

79   Do not mix waste materials collected from different processes before
      disposal unless the various components are known to be compatible,
      and only after considering the eventual disposal technique to be used.
      Any drums used for waste materials should be sound and not contain
      any incompatible residues. If a drum is being used as a collecting
      station for waste liquids, use a funnel that fits securely into the drum
      opening to reduce the possibility of spillage. There are funnels with lids
      and flame arresters to stop any external ignition from flashing back into
      the drum or to prevent the drum becoming dangerously pressurised if it

is engulfed by fire. When not in use containers of waste liquids should be securely closed to prevent leakage and returned to storage areas or cabinets. Do not add anything to waste liquid containers in storage areas (see paragraph 22), but bring the can or drum out to a designated work area.

80   Recovering waste liquid by distillation or other means may be feasible, particularly where large amounts are involved. Proprietary batch stills with a capacity of a few hundred litres are available, and larger amounts can be sent to a specialist firm for recovery. Seek specialist advice if the solvents to be recovered contain unstable residues such as nitro-cellulose.

81   Close drums and other containers that have been used to hold flammable liquids but have not been thoroughly cleaned and store them in a safe place before disposal or re-use. The standard of storage should be the same as that for full containers (see HS(G)51)[11]. Provide appropriate labels for containers to be sent off-site, whether nominally empty or containing waste materials. The consignor should provide the operator of the vehicle with the necessary information (in writing) about the material to be carried, referring to the relevant carriage legislation[36,37,38]. Waste flammable liquids sent off-site will also be subject to environmental legislation including the Environmental Protection (Duty of Care) Regulations 1991[39] and the Controlled Waste (Registration of Carriers and Seizure of Vehicles) Regulations 1991[40].

INFORMATION AND TRAINING

82   Adequate training and a knowledge of the properties of flammable liquids are essential for their safe use and handling and are also requirements of the Management of Health and Safety at Work Regulations 1992[1]. Carrying out the risk assessments required by these Regulations will identify how much information, training and retraining are needed. Further guidance on these Regulations is contained in the Approved Code of Practice entitled *Management of health and safety at work*[41].

83   All staff on the site should be informed of the hazards from the
      flammable liquids in use there, and of the need to exclude sources of
      ignition and heat from designated areas. Those handling flammable
      liquids or working on plant containing flammable liquids should also
      receive specific training in both normal operating procedures and
      emergency procedures. Periodic retraining will usually be needed.
      The training should cover the following:

- the types of flammable liquids in use, their properties and
  hazards;
- general procedures for safe handling of liquids and operation of
  plant;
- use of protective clothing;
- housekeeping;
- reporting of faults and incidents, including minor leaks and
  spills;
- specific instructions on individual items of plant and processes;
- emergency procedures, including raising the alarm, and use of
  appropriate fire-fighting equipment.

There should be written procedures for controlling the risks from the
use and handling of flammable liquids, and these should be used as a
basis for training.

GENERAL FIRE PRECAUTIONS

84   The possibility of a fire and its uncontrolled escalation can be
      minimised by:

- good plant design and layout;
- sound engineering;
- good operating practice;
- proper instruction of workers in routine operations and in the
  action to be taken in an emergency.

However, to ensure that people are able to evacuate the plant or buildings safely by their own unaided efforts in the event of a fire, the Fire Precautions Act 1971[42] requires the following:

☞ escape routes;
☞ means to enable these to be used;
☞ a system of giving warning in the case of fire;
☞ management procedures to ensure that all of the above are available and maintained, and that there is adequate training in their use.

The Fire Precautions Act 1971[42] is enforced by the Fire Authority, and for the majority of premises using flammable liquids the necessary provisions will be specified in a fire certificate issued by that Authority. Under the Fire Certificates (Special Premises) Regulations 1976[43], HSE issues the fire certificate for certain premises, including those handling large quantities of flammable liquids.

85   The Building Control Authorities' building Regulations specify the structural fire precautions and escape routes needed for new buildings and buildings undergoing major alteration and refurbishment. The authority issuing the fire certificate should be consulted about any fire precaution devices that can be conveniently installed during building or alteration work, such as fire alarms and fixed fire-fighting appliances. BS 5306 Part 3[44] contains advice on selecting, installing and maintaining portable fire extinguishers.

86   One of the requirements to ensure escape routes can be used is that fire extinguishers should be provided for tackling fires in their early stages. The presence of fire extinguishers should not make people delay their escape or postpone phoning the Fire Brigade. Works fire teams should not tackle fires that might place them at risk. The type of fire that such a team should tackle depends on the team's size and experience. Works fire teams should be trained to recognise when a fire is beyond their control and when it is likely to pose a threat to them.

87   The Fire Brigade on arrival will take responsibility for tackling fires.

Under the Fire Services Act 1947[45], they must make sure that whatever they need for fire-fighting is available, including water supplies and access for appliances. The firm and the Fire Authority should discuss these requirements, and the firm should inform the Authority of the materials and processes used on their premises. It should also arrange for people familiar with these to be on hand to advise Fire Brigade staff in case of an emergency. Contact names can be given to the site security or contact numbers posted at the entrance to the site.

88   Consider protecting valuable plant from fire, either actively or passively, to limit the damage caused by any incident. BS 5908[46] gives further guidance, or specialist advice can be obtained.

EMERGENCY PROCEDURES

89   Putting safety measures into practice at the earliest stage can significantly reduce the impact of an incident on people and premises. A procedure for dealing with fires, spills or leaks should therefore be drawn up to cover:

- raising the alarm;
- calling the Fire Brigade;
- tackling the fire or controlling a spill or leak (when it is safe to do so);
- shutting down the plant safely;
- evacuating the plant safely.

Where large numbers of employees on site or people off site may be at risk, one person should be nominated to draw up an action plan, liaise with other services and decide on the appropriate scale of response.

90   Where foreseeable incidents may affect people or property beyond the site boundary, the emergency services should be consulted when preparing the emergency procedures. Formal on-site and off-site emergency plans are required at sites subject to regulations 7 to12 of the Control of Industrial Major Accident Hazard (CIMAH) Regulations 1984[47] - see HS(G)25[48].

APPENDIX 1: LEGAL REQUIREMENTS

Health and Safety at Work etc Act 1974[2]

1   This Act is concerned with securing the health, safety and welfare of people at work and with protecting those who are not at work from risks to their health and safety arising from work activities. The Act and its relevant statutory provisions also deal with controlling the storage and use of explosives and highly flammable or otherwise dangerous substances. The general duties in sections 2 to 4 and 6 to 8 of this Act apply to all the work activities which are the subject of this guidance book. The Act is enforced either by HSE or by local authorities as determined by the Health and Safety (Enforcing Authority) Regulations 1989[49]. Guidance on the Act is contained in an HSE publication entitled *A guide to the Health and Safety at Work etc Act 1974*[50].

Management of Health and Safety at Work Regulations 1992[1]

2   These Regulations require all employers and self-employed persons to assess the risks to workers and others who may be affected by their undertakings so that they can decide what measures need to be taken to fulfil their statutory obligations. These Regulations also require an assessment to decide on appropriate health and safety arrangements, health surveillance, emergency planning, and the provision of information and training. An Approved Code of Practice gives guidance on the provisions of these Regulations[41].

Highly Flammable Liquids and Liquefied Petroleum Gases Regulations 1972[3]

3   These Regulations apply when liquids which have a flashpoint of less than 32°C and which support combustion (when tested in the prescribed manner) are present at premises subject to the Factories Act 1961[51]. The Regulations include provisions for these highly flammable liquids relating to:

- ☞   precautions to be taken during storage;
- ☞   precautions to be taken against spills and leaks;

- controls for sources of ignition in areas where accumulations of vapours might occur;
- means to prevent the escape of vapours;
- dispersal of dangerous concentrations of vapours;
- controls on smoking.

An exception to the storage requirements of these Regulations applies where a petroleum licence is in force. Highly flammable liquids defined by these Regulations are included in the scope of this guidance document.

Factories Act 1961[51]

4   The Act defines a 'factory' and contains many general and detailed provisions relating to work activities in factories. Section 31(3) contains specific requirements relating to the opening of plant that contains any explosive or inflammable gas or vapour under pressure, and Section 31(4) contains specific requirements relating to the application of heat to plant that has contained any explosive or inflammable substance. 'Inflammable' means able to burn with a flame and 'flammable' is generally taken to have the same meaning as 'inflammable'. Inflammable substances and vapours will include flammable liquids and their vapours as defined in this guidance document.

Petroleum (Consolidation) Act 1928[5]

5   The Act defines petroleum and petroleum spirit and requires the keeping of such liquids (except for small specified quantities) to be authorised by a licence, and to be in accordance with any conditions of the licence. The Petroleum (Mixtures) Order 1929[6] extends these requirements to petroleum mixtures which are defined in the Order.

Chemicals (Hazard Information and Packaging for Supply) Regulations 1994[4]

6   These Regulations, commonly referred to as the CHIPS Regulations,

contain requirements for the supply of chemicals. The Regulations
require the supplier of chemicals to:

☞   classify them, that is, identify their hazards;

☞   give information about the hazards to the people they supply,
      both in the form of labels and safety data sheets;

☞   package the chemicals safely.

Classifying chemicals according to the CHIPS Regulations requires
knowledge of physical and chemical properties, including the
flashpoints of liquids, and of health and environmental effects.
Chemicals are grouped into three categories of danger, according to
their flashpoints:

☞   extremely flammable - those liquids with a flashpoint lower than
      0°C and a boiling point lower than or equal to 35°C;

☞   highly flammable - liquids which have a flashpoint below 21°C
      but are not extremely flammable;

☞   flammable liquids - liquids which have a flashpoint equal to or
      greater than 21°C and less than or equal to 55°C and which
      support combustion when tested in the prescribed manner at
      55°C.

Flammable, highly flammable and extremely flammable liquids are all
included in the scope of this guidance book. The Regulations are
supported by an Approved supply list[52] containing agreed classifications
for some common substances, an approved classification and labelling
guide, an Approved Code of Practice on safety data sheets and by the
guidance publication *CHIP 2 for everyone*[53].

**Carriage of Dangerous Goods by Road and Rail (Classification,
Packaging and Labelling) Regulations 1994**[36]

7   These Regulations apply to the transportation of dangerous goods by
      road and rail. Their aim is to reduce the hazards involved in
      transporting such substances by requiring them to be correctly

classified, and packaged and labelled according to that classification. They specify that dangerous substances should be carried in suitable containers which will not leak under normal handling; these should bear appropriate warning labels giving information on the nature of the hazards. Two associated documents, the *Approved carriage list*[54] and the *Approved methods for the classification and packaging of dangerous goods for carriage by road and rail*[55] provide assistance to enable compliance with these Regulations. Flammable liquids classified as dangerous substances by these Regulations are those liquids which have a flashpoint of 61°C or below (with certain exceptions based on their combustibility) or liquids with a flashpoint above 61°C carried at temperatures above their flashpoint. Flammable liquids defined in this guidance will be included in the scope of these Regulations.

Road Traffic (Carriage of Dangerous Substances in Road Tankers and Tank Containers) Regulations 1992[37] and the Road Traffic (Carriage of Dangerous Substances in Packages etc) Regulations 1992[38]

8   These Regulations complement the Carriage of Dangerous Goods by Road and Rail (Classification, Packaging and Labelling) Regulations 1994[36]. Their provisions include requirements for:

☞   the construction of vehicles;
☞   information to be received by operators and to be given to drivers;
☞   the marking of vehicles;
☞   the loading, stowage and unloading of consignments.

Dangerous substances are those materials included in the Approved Carriage List[54] produced in association with the 1994 Regulations or with the characteristic properties defined in Schedule 1 of those Regulations or Schedule 1 of the road tanker Regulations[37]. The 1992 road tanker Regulations define a flammable liquid as having a flashpoint of 55°C and below, but these will be revised to bring the classification into line with the above 1994 carriage Regulations.

Flammable liquids defined in this guidance will be included in the scope of these Regulations.

Electricity at Work Regulations 1989[22]

9   These Regulations impose requirements for electrical systems and equipment, including work activities on or near electrical equipment. They also require electrical equipment which is exposed to any flammable or explosive substance, including flammable liquids or vapours, to be constructed or protected so as to prevent danger. Advice is available in HS(R)25[56].

Notification of Installations Handling Hazardous Substances Regulations (NIHHS) 1982[57]

10   These Regulations require premises with specified quantities of particular substances, such as 10 000 tonnes or more of flammable liquids with a flashpoint of less than 21°C to be notified to HSE. Following the Planning (Hazardous Substances) Act 1990[58] and Regulations 1992[59], the presence of NIHHS Schedule 1 substances and quantities, together with some from CIMAH Schedule 3[47], on, over or under land requires consent from hazardous substances authorities. Similar provisions also apply in Scotland.

Control of Industrial Major Accident Hazards Regulations 1984 as amended 1989/90[47]

11   These Regulations apply at two levels to certain premises where specified quantities of particular substances are stored or used, such as flammable liquids with a flashpoint below 21°C and a boiling point (at normal pressure) above 20°C. The main aim of these Regulations is to prevent major accidents occurring; a secondary objective is to limit the effects of any which do happen. A major accident is a major emission, fire or explosion resulting from uncontrolled developments which leads to serious danger to people or the environment. The first level requirements apply at premises where 5000 tonnes or more of

flammable liquids, as defined above, are involved in certain industrial activities, including processing operations and storage. The second level requirements apply where 50 000 tonnes or more of flammable liquids are involved. The general requirements apply at both levels and require the person in control of the industrial activity to demonstrate that the major accident hazards have been identified and that the activity is being operated safely. The additional requirements that apply at the second level include the submission of a written safety report, preparation of an on-site emergency plan and provision of certain information for the public. HS(R)21[60] gives guidance on these Regulations.

Control of Substances Hazardous to Health Regulations 1994[9]

12   These Regulations require employers to assess the risks arising from hazardous substances at work and to decide on the measures needed to protect the health of employees. The employer is also required to take appropriate action to prevent or adequately control exposure to the hazardous substance. Substances covered by the Regulations include carcinogenic substances and those which, under the Chemicals (Hazard Information and Packaging for Supply) Regulations 1994[4], are labelled as very toxic, toxic, harmful, corrosive or irritant. The Regulations also cover dusts, where present in substantial quantities, and those substances assigned occupational exposure limits. Flammable liquids normally have toxic or harmful properties which bring them within the scope of these Regulations.

Safety Signs Regulations 1980[61]

13   These Regulations contain requirements for safety signs giving health and safety information or instructions to people at work (except for certain circumstances described in the Regulations) to comply with Part 1 of BS 5378[12]. A Safety Signs Directive (92/58/EEC) to be implemented by European Community Member States will result in these Regulations being replaced by the new Health and Safety (Safety Signs and Signals) Regulations. The Directive lays down a requirement

to provide, maintain and use a sign when risk assessment has indicated the need for a sign to warn of a hazard that cannot be prevented or controlled effectively by other means. Annexes I to VII of the Directive contain details of appropriate signs. Generally, the signs that are included in BS 5378[12] will meet the requirements of the Directive.

Provision and Use of Work Equipment Regulations 1992[62]

14   These Regulations implement a European Community Directive and aim to ensure the provision of safe work equipment and its safe use. They include general duties covering the selection of suitable equipment, maintenance, information, instructions and training, and they also address the need for equipment to be able to control selected hazards. Regulation 12 is particularly relevant to equipment associated with flammable liquids. It requires employers to ensure that people using work equipment are not exposed to hazards arising from:

- equipment catching fire or overheating;
- the unintended or premature discharge of any liquid or vapour;
- the unintended or premature explosion of the work equipment or any substance used or stored in it.

Guidance on these Regulations is available in an HSE publication entitled *Work equipment*[63].

Fire Precautions Act 1971[42]

15   This Act controls what have become known as the 'General Fire Precautions', covering the means of escape in case of fire, the means for ensuring the escape routes can be used safely and effectively, the means for fighting fires, and the means for giving warning in the case of fire; and the training of staff in fire safety. The Act allows the presence of flammable liquids to be taken into account when considering general fire precautions. The Act is enforced by the Fire Authorities and further guidance can be found in a Home Office publication entitled *Guide to fire precautions in existing places of work that require a fire certificate - factories, offices, shops and railway premises*[64].

Fire Certificate (Special Premises) Regulations 1976[43]

16   These Regulations apply at premises where certain quantities of hazardous materials are processed, used or stored. For flammable liquids they apply at premises where there is a total of more than 4000 tonnes of any highly flammable liquid (as defined by the Highly Flammable Liquids and Liquefied Petroleum Gases Regulations 1972[3]) or more than 50 tonnes of any highly flammable liquid held under pressure greater than atmospheric pressure and at a temperature above its boiling point. Where these Regulations apply they take the place of the Fire Precautions Act 1971[42] and designate HSE as the enforcing authority for matters relating to general fire precautions.

Dangerous Substances (Notification and Marking of Sites) Regulations 1990[65]

17   The purpose of these Regulations is to assist the fire-fighting services by the provision of advance and on-site information on sites containing large quantities of dangerous substances. The Regulations apply at sites containing total quantities of 25 tonnes or more of dangerous substances. Dangerous substances include flammable liquids with a flashpoint below 55°C as defined by this guidance document. The Regulations require suitable signs to be erected at access points and at any locations specified by an inspector, and notification to the appropriate fire and enforcing authorities of the presence of any dangerous substances. HS(R)29[66] gives further guidance.

APPENDIX 2: FIRE-RESISTING STRUCTURES

HM Chief Inspector of Factories has issued Certificate of Approval No 1 for storerooms, process cabinets or enclosures, workrooms, cupboards, bins, ducts, and casings, which are required to be fire-resisting under the Highly Flammable Liquids and Liquefied Petroleum Gases Regulations 1972[3]. The main requirements for cabinets, enclosures, workrooms, ducts and casings are summarised below. These should form the basis for construction of fire-resisting enclosures, whether or not the specific Regulations apply.

1   **Cabinets and enclosures**

(a) (i)   Each side, top, floor and door should be half-hour fire-resistant to BS 476[67] Part 8 (now replaced by Parts 20 and 22).

(ii) The internal surface material (and any substrate to which it is bonded) should, if tested to BS 476 Part 6 (fire propagation test), have a performance index of not more than 12 and a sub-index of not more than 6.

Exceptions to (i) and (ii) are fume cabinets and glove boxes, and ovens used only for evaporating solvents from materials.

(b) Each side, top, floor and door should be supported and fastened to prevent failure of the structure in a fire for at least half an hour. Supports and fastenings should be non-combustible to BS 476 Part 4. Exceptions are fume cabinets and glove boxes.

(c) The joins between sides, tops and floors should be bonded or fire-stopped to prevent or retard the passage of flame and hot gases.

(d) The structure should be robust enough to withstand foreseeable accidental damage.

(e)   If the surfaces of the structure are liable to be coated with residues, the structure should allow removal of the residues without impairing its fire resistance or its ability to resist flame spread.

(f)   Each side, top, floor and door of ovens used only for solvent evaporation should be non-combustible if tested to BS 476 Part 4.

2   **Workrooms**

Note: The following requirements do not apply to external doors, windows and walls, ventilation openings, or to tops or ceilings of single-storey buildings and top-floor rooms.

(a)   Each enclosing element, for example, walls, doors, windows, floors and ceilings should be half-hour fire-resistant to BS 476 Part 8 (now replaced by Parts 20-23), except for a floor immediately above the ground. The insulation requirement is waived for floors, ceilings and doors.

(b)   All internal surfaces should be at least Class 1 if tested to BS 476 Part 7 (surface spread of flame), except for floors and doors, and windows and their frames.

(c)   Doors should be self-closing from any position.

(d)   Joins between elements of construction should be bonded or fire-stopped to prevent or retard the passage of flame and hot gases.

(e)   The structure should be robust enough to withstand foreseeable accidental damage.

(f)   If the surfaces of the structure are liable to be coated with residues, the structure should allow for removal of the residues without impairing its fire resistance or its ability to resist flame spread.

3 **Ducts, trunks and casings**

(a) Ducts, trunks and casings should be able to satisfy BS 476 Part 8 (now replaced by Parts 20 and 22) in remaining free from collapse and resisting the passage of flame for at least half an hour.

(b) The internal surface material (and any substrate to which it is bonded) should, if tested to BS 476 Part 6 (fire propagation test), have a performance index of not more than 12 and a sub-index of not more than 6.

(c) The structure should be robust enough to withstand foreseeable accidental damage.

(d) If the surfaces of the structure are liable to be coated with residues, the structure should allow removal of the residues without impairing its fire resistance or its ability to resist flame spread.

(e) Ducts, trunks and casings should be supported and fastened to prevent failure of the structure in an internal fire for at least half an hour. Supports and fastenings should be non-combustible to BS 476 Part 4.

APPENDIX 3: HAZARDOUS AREA CLASSIFICATION

1   The first approach should always be to control the use of flammable
materials (that is, liquids above their flashpoint, gases and vapours) by
adopting suitable precautions, so as to minimise the extent of any
hazardous area. The concept of hazardous area classification has, in the
past, been used solely as the basis for selecting fixed electrical
apparatus. However, it also can be used to help eliminate potential
ignition sources, including portable electrical equipment, vehicles, hot
surfaces, etc, from flammable atmospheres.

2   Hazardous areas fall into three types of zone: Zone 0, Zone 1 and Zone
2, which are three-dimensional spaces in which flammable
concentrations of vapours may be present. The higher the zone number
the lower the likelihood that a flammable vapour will exist within the
zone. Electrical equipment suitable for use in Zone 0 is produced to a
higher specification (that is, it is less likely to produce an incendive
spark on failure) than that suitable for use in Zone 1, which in turn is
produced to a higher standard than that for use in Zone 2. The aim is to
reduce to an acceptable minimum level the probability of a flammable
atmosphere coinciding with an electrical or other source of ignition.
The three zones are defined as follows:

(a)   ***Zone 0 - An area in which an explosive gas-air mixture is
continuously present, or present for long periods.*** A Zone 0
classification applies to enclosed spaces which are likely to
contain a flammable vapour continuously or for long periods.
Examples are the inside of process vessels and storage
containers. It may also apply in the immediate vicinity of
exposed liquid surfaces and of continuous releases of flammable
material.

(b)   ***Zone 1 - An area in which an explosive gas-air mixture is likely
to occur in normal operation.*** A Zone 1 classification will be
appropriate if either of the following apply:

    (i)   The area contains plant which may, in normal operation, release sufficient flammable material to create a hazard.

    (ii)   The area fulfils the requirements for Zone 2 but the ventilation or drainage are inadequate to ensure a flammable atmosphere is quickly dispersed. This is likely to apply to pits, trenches and similar depressions in the case of heavier-than-air gases and to enclosed roof spaces for lighter-than-air gases.

(c)   ***Zone 2 - An area in which an explosive gas-air mixture is not likely to occur in normal operation, and if it occurs it will exist only for a short time.*** A Zone 2 classification can be applied if all of the following are satisfied:

    (i)   In normal operation, there is no flammable liquid in direct contact with the surrounding atmosphere.

    (ii)   The plant concerned is constructed, installed and maintained so as to prevent, in normal operation, the release of sufficient flammable material to create a hazard.

    (iii)   The area is well enough ventilated and drained to disperse any flammable atmosphere quickly in the event of a release, so that any contact with electrical apparatus is only for a brief period.

(d)   Areas outside these zones are defined as non-hazardous.

3   If the temperature of a liquid is not likely to be raised above its flashpoint, and there is little likelihood of a flammable mist or spray occurring, the liquid may be considered not to give rise to a hazardous area. Explosion protection of electrical equipment is not then required, but steps should be taken to prevent leaks or splashes of the liquid from coming into contact with electrical equipment. Nonetheless, there should be no likelihood of local heating of the liquid, which might produce a flammable vapour. High flashpoint liquids subject to

temperatures above their flashpoint should be treated as flammable liquids. In case of doubt seek specialist advice.

4 A plan should be drawn up showing the allocation of zones to each part of the premises. The extent of each zone will vary with the layout of the building, the design of the plant, ventilation at the plant and the type of materials handled. Further advice is available from industry codes, BS 5345[18] Part 2 and the Institute of Petroleum *Model code of safe practice in the petroleum industry: Part 15: Area classification code*[68].

Notes

1 Pipework with all-welded joints is not normally a source of hazard provided the risk of damage is negligible.

2 Allow for routine releases of small amounts of flammable material in a Zone 2 area, for example during sampling, by assigning a small Zone 1 area around the point of release.

3 Regular emissions of flammable vapour, for example from tank vents during pumping, will likewise give rise to a Zone 1 area around each point of release.

Item	Extent of area	Classification
Pump (inside a building)	a) within any enclosure around the pump	Zone 1
	b) within a horizontal radius of 4 m and vertically from the ground level to 2 m above the unit	Zone 2
Closed process vessel, filled and emptied by pipeline	a) Inside the vessel	Zone 0
	b) Vertically from ground level to 2 m above the vessel and horizontally to 2 m from the vessel (or to 1 m outside the sill if this is greater)	Zone 2
Open vessel	a) Inside the vessel	Zone 0
	b) Vertically from ground level to 1 m above the vessel and horizontally to 2 m from the vessel	Zone 1
	c) Horizontally to 2 m beyond the Zone 1 area (or to 1 m outside the sill if this is greater). Also vertically to a height of 3 m if the Zone 1 area does not reach 3 m in height	Zone 2
Metered discharge point	a) within 2 m horizontally of the discharge point and from floor level to 1 m above the source	Zone 1
	b) horizontally to 2 m beyond the Zone 1 boundary, (or to 1 m outside the sill if this is greater), and vertically to a height of 3 m if the Zone 1 area does not reach 3 m in height	Zone 2

Table 1 Typical hazardous area classification

GLOSSARY

Auto-ignition temperature: The minimum temperature at which a material will ignite spontaneously under specified test conditions. Also referred to as minimum ignition temperature.

Combustible: Capable of burning in air when ignited.

Enforcing authority: The authority with responsibility for enforcing the Health and Safety at Work etc Act 1974[2] and other relevant statutory provisions.

Fire-resisting: Able to fulfil, for a stated period of time, the required stability, fire integrity and/or thermal insulation, where appropriate, in a standard fire resistance test. See Appendix 2.

Flame arrester: A device consisting of an element, a housing and associated fittings which is constructed and used to prevent the passage of flame. An arrester may be categorised as either an end-of-line deflagration arrester, an in-line deflagration arrester or a detonation arrester - see BS 7244[20] for requirements and test methods. Most flame arresters consist of an assembly containing narrow passages or apertures through which gases or vapours can flow but which are too small for a flame to pass through.

Flammable: Capable of burning with a flame. See paragraph 4 for the definition of 'flammable liquid' used in this guidance.

Flammable range: The concentration of a flammable vapour in air falling between the upper and lower explosion limits.

Flashpoint: The minimum temperature at which a liquid, under specific test conditions, gives off sufficient flammable vapour to ignite momentarily on the application of an ignition source.

Hazard: Anything with the potential for causing harm. The harm may be to people, property or the environment, and may result from substances, machines, methods of work or work organisation.

Hazardous area: An area where flammable or explosive gas or vapour-air mixtures (often referred to as explosive gas-air mixtures) are, or may be expected to be, present in quantities which require special precautions to be taken against the risk of ignition. See Appendix 3.

Incendive: Having sufficient energy to ignite a flammable mixture.

Inert: Incapable of supporting combustion; to render incapable of supporting combustion.

Lower explosion limit (LEL): The minimum concentration of vapour in air below which the propagation of a flame will not occur in the presence of an ignition source. Also referred to as the lower flammable limit or the lower explosive limit.

Non-combustible material: A material that fulfils the criteria for non-combustibility given in BS 476[67] Part 4: 1970. Alternatively, a material which, when tested in accordance with BS 476 Part 11: 1982, does not flame and gives no rise in temperature on either the centre or furnace thermocouples.

Risk: The likelihood that, should an incident occur, harm from a particular hazard will affect a specified population. Risk reflects both the likelihood that harm will occur and its severity in relation to the numbers of people who might be affected, and the consequences to them.

Risk assessment: The process of identifying the hazards present in any undertaking (whether arising from work activities or other factors) and those likely to be affected by them, and of evaluating the extent of the risks involved, bearing in mind whatever precautions are already being taken.

Upper explosion limit (UEL): The maximum concentration of vapour in air above which the propagation of a flame will not occur. Also referred to as the upper flammable limit or the upper explosive limit.

Vapour: The gaseous phase released by evaporation from a material that is a liquid at normal temperatures and pressure.

Zone: The classified part of a hazardous area, representing the probability of a flammable vapour (or gas) and air mixture being present. See Appendix 3.

REFERENCES AND FURTHER READING

References

1   *Management of Health and Safety at Work Regulations 1992* SI 1992/2051 HMSO 1992 ISBN 0 11 025051 6

2   *Health and Safety at Work etc Act 1974* Ch 37 HMSO 1974 ISBN 0 10 543774 3

3   *Highly Flammable Liquids and Liquefied Petroleum Gases Regulations 1972* SI 1972/917 HMSO 1972 ISBN 0 11 020917 6

4   *Chemicals (Hazard Information and Packaging for Supply) Regulations 1994* SI 1994/3247 HMSO 1994 ISBN 0 11 043877 9

5   *Petroleum (Consolidation) Act 1928* Chapter 32 HMSO 1928

6   *Petroleum (Mixtures) Order 1929* HMSO 1929 ISBN 0 11 100031 9

7   *Environmental Protection Act 1990* HMSO 1990 ISBN 0 10 544390 5

8   HSE *Safety datasheets for substances and preparations dangerous for supply* Guidance on Regulation 6 of the CHIP Regulations 1994 Approved Code of Practice L62 HSE Books 1995 ISBN 0 7176 0859 X

9   *Control of Substances Hazardous to Health Regulations 1994* SI 1994/3246 HMSO 1994 ISBN 0 11 043721 7

10 HSE *Storage of packaged dangerous substances* HS(G)71 HSE Books 1992 ISBN 0 11 885989 7

11 HSE *The storage of flammable liquids in containers* HS(G)51 HSE Books 1990 ISBN 0 7176 0481 0

12 British Standards Institution *Safety signs and colours* BS 5378: 1980

13   American National Standards Institute Standard B31.3 *Chemical plant and petroleum refinery piping* (with addenda)

      1   1981 addenda to ANSI/ASME B31.3 - 1990 edition (AWSI/ASME)
      2   1982 addenda to ANSI/ASME B31.3 - 1990 edition (AWS1/ASME B31.3b - 1980)

14   Engineering Equipment and Material Users Association Supplement 153 to ANSI/ASME B31.3 1989

15   British Standards Institution *Specification for pipe supports* BS 3974: 1974

16   British Standards Institution *Code of practice for the identification of pipelines* BS CP 1710: 1971

17   British Standards Institution *Code of practice for accommodation of building services in ducts* BS 8313:1989

18   British Standards Institution *Code of practice for the selection, installation and maintenance of electrical apparatus for use in potentially explosive atmospheres* BS 5345: 1989 (in 8 parts)

19   European Code of Practice *Electrical installations in potentially explosive gas atmospheres (other than mines)* prEN 50154 (also published under the same title as International Standard IEC 79-14)

20   British Standards Institution *Flame arresters for general use* BS 7244:1990

21   HSE *Health and safety in motor vehicle repair* HSE Books 1991 HS(G)67 ISBN 0 11 885671 5

22   *Electricity at Work Regulations 1989* SI 1989/635 HMSO 1989 ISBN 0 11 096635 X

23   Institution of Chemical Engineers *Electricity and flammable substances: A short guide for small businesses* ISBN 0 85 295250 3 1989

24   British Standards Institution *Code of practice for earthing* BS 7430:1991

25   British Standards Institution *Code of practice for the control of undesirable static electricity* BS 5958
Part 1: 1980 General considerations
Part 2 : 1983 Recommendations for particular industrial situations

26   British Standards Institution *Specification for lined industrial vulcanised rubber boots* BS 5145: 1989

27   British Standards Institution *Specification for lined lightweight rubber overshoes and overboots* BS 7193: 1989

28   HSE *Diesel-engined lift trucks in hazardous areas* PM 58 HSE Books 1986 ISBN 0 11 883535 1

29   HSE *The cleaning and gas freeing of tanks containing flammable residues* CS 15 HSE Books 1985 ISBN 0 11 883518 1

30   HSC Oil Industry Advisory Committee *Guidance on permit-to-work systems in the petroleum industry* HSE Books 1991 ISBN 0 11 885688 X

31   HSE *Occupational exposure limits* EH 40/95 HSE Books 1995 ISBN 0 7176 0876 X

32   HSE *Spraying of highly flammable liquids* EH 9 HSE Books 1977 ISBN 0 11 883034 1

33   HSE *Evaporating and other ovens* HS(G)16 HSE Books 1981 ISBN 0 11 883433 9

34   HSC *General COSHH ACoP, Carcinogens ACoP* and *Biological agents
      ACoP:Control of Substances Hazardous to Health Regulations 1994*
      HSE Books 1995 ISBN 0 7176 0819 0

35   HSE *Dangerous maintenance - a study of maintenance accidents and
      how to prevent them* HSE Books 1992 ISBN 0 11 886347 9

36   HSE *Carriage of Dangerous Goods by Road and Rail (Classification,
      Packaging and Labelling) Regulations 1994* SI 1994/669 HMSO 1994
      ISBN 0 11 043669 5

37   HSE *Road Traffic (Carriage of Dangerous Substances in Road Tankers
      and Tank Containers) Regulations 1992* SI 1992/743 HMSO 1992
      ISBN 0 11 023743 9

38   HSE *Road Traffic (Carriage of Dangerous Substances in Packages,
      etc) Regulations 1992* SI 1992/742 HMSO 1992 ISBN 0 11 023742 0

39   *Environmental Protection (Duty of Care) Regulations 1991*
      SI 1991/2839 HMSO 1991 ISBN 0 11 015853 9

40   *Controlled Waste (Registration of Carriers and Seizure of Vehicles)
      Regulations 1991* SI 1991/1624 HMSO 1991 ISBN 0 11 014624 7

41   HSC *Management of Health and Safety at Work* The Management of
      Health and Safety at Work Regulations 1992 Approved Code of
      Practice L21 HSE Books 1992 ISBN 0 7176 0412 8

42   Home Office and Scottish Office *Fire Precautions Act 1971* Ch 40
      HMSO 1971 ISBN 0 10 544071 X

43   *Fire Certificates (Special Premises) Regulations 1976* SI 1976/2003
      HMSO 1976 ISBN 0 11 062003 8

44   British Standards Institution BS 5306 *Code of practice for fire extinguishing installations and equipment on premises*
Part 1: 1976 *Hydrant systems, hose reels and foam inlets*
Part 3: 1985 *Code of practice for the selection, installation and maintenance of portable fire extinguishers*

45   *Fire Services Act 1947* Ch 41 HMSO 1947 ISBN 0 10 850109 4

46   British Standards Institution BS 5908: 1990 *Code of practice for fire precautions in the chemical and allied industries* ISBN 0 58 018205 3

47   *Control of Industrial Major Accident Hazards Regulations 1984* SI 1984/1902 HMSO ISBN 0 11 047902 5

48   HSE *Control of Industrial Major Accident Hazards Regulations 1984 (CIMAH):Further guidance on emergency plans* HS(G)25 HSE Books 1985 ISBN 0 11 883831 8

49   *Health and Safety (Enforcing Authority) Regulations 1989* SI 1989/1903 HMSO 1989 ISBN 0 11 097903 6

50   HSE *A guide to the Health and Safety at Work etc Act 1974* HSE Books 1992 ISBN 0 7176 0441 1

51   *Factories Act 1961* Chapter 34 HMSO 1961 ISBN 0 10 850027 6

52   HSE *Approved supply list and database - CHIP 2* L61 ISBN 0 7176 0858 1

53   HSE *CHIP 2 for everyone* HS(G)126 HSE Books 1995 ISBN 0 7176 0857 3

54   HSE *Approved carriage list: Information approved for the classification, packaging and labelling of dangerous goods for carriage by road and rail*   L57 HSE BOOKS 1994 ISBN 0 7176 0745 3

55   HSE *Approved methods for the classification and packaging of dangerous goods for carriage by road and rail*   HSE Books 1994 ISBN 0 7176 0744 5

56   HSE *Memorandum of guidance on the Electricity at Work Regulations 1989* HS(R)25 HSE Books 1989 ISBN 0 11 883963 2

57   *Notification of Installations Handling Hazardous Substances Regulations 1982* SI 1982/1357 HMSO 1982 ISBN 0 11 027357 5

58   *Planning (Hazardous Substances) Act 1990* HMSO 1990 ISBN 0 10 541090 X

59   *Planning (Hazardous Substances) Regulations 1992* SI 1992/656 HMSO 1992 ISBN 0 11 023656 4

60   HSE *A guide to the Control of Industrial Major Accident Hazards Regulations 1984* HS(R)21 HSE Books 1990 ISBN 0 11 885579 4

61   *Safety Signs Regulations 1980*   SI 1980/1471 HMSO 1980 ISBN 0 11 007471 8

62   *Provision and Use of Work Equipment Regulations 1992*   SI 1992/2932 HMSO 1992 ISBN 0 11 025849 5

63   HSE *Work equipment*   Provision and Use of Work Equipment Regulations 1992 Guidance on Regulations L22 HSE Books 1992 ISBN 0 7176 0414 4

64   Home Office/Scottish Home and Health Department *Guide to fire precautions in existing places of work that require a fire certificate - factories, offices, shops and railway premises* HMSO 1993 ISBN 0 11 341079 4

65   *Dangerous Substances (Notification and Marking of Sites) Regulations 1990* SI 1990/304 HMSO 1990 ISBN 0 11 003304 3

66   HSE *Notification and marking of sites* Dangerous Substances (Notification and Marking of Sites) Regulations 1990 HS(R)29 HSE Books 1990 ISBN 0 11 885435 6

67   British Standards Institution BS 476 *Fire tests on building materials and structures* (in various parts)

68   Institute of Petroleum *Model code of safe practice in the petroleum industry Part 15: Area classification code* 1990 ISBN 0 47 192160 2

Further reading

British Standards Institution BS 5274:1985 *Specification for fire hose reels (water) for fixed installations*

Chemical Industries Association *Guidelines for bulk handling of ethylene oxide* 1983

Chemical Recovery Association *Code of Practice for the recovery of flammable solvents* 1977

Drinks National Industry Group *Storage and handling of high strength potable alcohol*

Fire Protection Association *Compendium of fire safety data* Volume 2 *Industrial and process fire safety*

Fire Protection Association *Fire and related properties of industrial chemicals 1972*

HSE *Dispensing petrol: Assessing and controlling the risk of fire and explosion at sites where petrol is stored and dispensed as a fuel* HS(G)146 HSE Books 1996 ISBN 0 7176 1048 9

HSE *The storage of flammable liquids in fixed tanks (up to 10 000m³ total capacity)* HS(G)50 HSE Books 1990 ISBN 0 11 885532 8

HSE *The storage of flammable liquids in fixed tanks (exceeding 10 000m³ total capacity)* HS(G)52 HSE Books 1991 ISBN 0 11 885538 7

The Petroleum - Spirit (Plastic Containers) Regulations 1982 SI 1982/630 HMSO ISBN 0 11 026630 7

HSE *Approved guide to the classification and labelling of substances and preparations dangerous for supply - CHIP 2* L63 HSE Books 1995 ISBN 0 7176 0860 3

HSE *The storage and handling of organic peroxides* CS 21 HSE Books 1991 ISBN 0 11 885602 2

HSE *Entry into confined spaces* GS 5 HSE Books 1994 ISBN 0 7176 0787 9

HSE *Loading and unloading of bulk flammable liquids and gases at harbours and inland waterways* GS 40 HSE Books 1986 ISBN 0 11 883931 4

HSC *Fire safety in the printing industry* HSE Books 1992 ISBN 0 11 886375 4

HSE *Glass reinforced plastic vessels and tanks: Advice to users* PM 75 HSE Books 1991 ISBN 0 11 885608 1

HSE priced and free publications can be obtained by mail order from HSE Books (see back cover for details). HSE priced publications are also available from good booksellers.

British Standards are available from:
389 Chiswick High Road, London W4 9AL
Tel: 0181 996 7000
Fax: 0181 996 7001

Printed in the UK for the Health and Safety Executive   C70   1/96

SAFE USE AND HANDLING OF FLAMMABLE LIQUIDS
Reader feedback questionnaire

To help us produce guidance which is easy to follow, informative and effective, it would help greatly if you could complete and return this questionnaire. Your views on the guidance are important, and help us improve future publications. When the questionnaire is completed please fold and return it to the prepaid address overleaf.

Name ....
Company / Organisation...
Address..
....
....
Postcode..

Size of Business? ☐
Self-employed ☐
Franchisee ☐
1 -10 employees ☐
11 -50 employees ☐
Over 50 employees ☐

Nature of business
Manufacturing ☐
Main activity ....
Government Local ☐
          Central ☐
Trade Association ☐
Trade Union ☐
Other ....

How did you hear of this publication?
Advertisement ☐   HSE Inspector ☐
Trade Association ☐   HSC Newsletter ☐
HSE Catalogue ☐   Mailshot ☐
Local Authority ☐   Informal business contact ☐
Other (Please specify)..
....
....

Did you find the guidance:

	Very useful			Not useful
	1	2	3	4

Was the text:

	Clear			Difficult
	1	2	3	4

Was the guidance presented:

	Well			Poorly
	1	2	3	4

Does the guidance represent:

	Good value			Poor value
	1	2	3	4

Does the guidance contain the information you need?   Yes   No

What other information did you expect it to contain?
....
....
....

How did you obtain this publication?

Direct from HSE Books on account	☐	Bought through Library	☐
Direct from HSE Books by mail order	☐	Sent by HSE Inspector	☐
Bought from Bookshop on account	☐	Sent by Consultant	☐
Bought from Bookshop by cash sale	☐	Copy belonging to a colleague	☐
Bookshop name...................................		Don't know	☐

Thank you for taking the time to answer these questions

BUSINESS REPLY SERVICE
Licence No. LV 5189

Health and Safety Executive
Room 303, Daniel House
Stanley Precinct
Bootle
Merseyside
L20 3QY

FLIQ

FIRST FOLD

SECOND FOLD

THIRD FOLD

FOURTH FOLD

B

A

Tuck A into B to form envelope
Please do not staple or glue

2